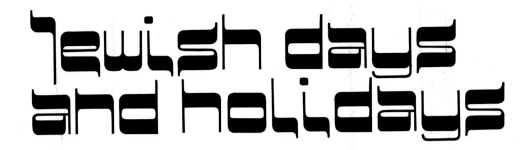

Jewish days and holidays

Greer Fay Cashman • Illustrated by Alona Frankel

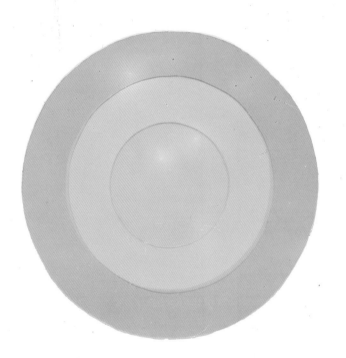

Adama Books, New York

© 1976 by Massada Press, Jerusalem
© 1986, USA edition, by Adama Books

Designed by Magda Tsfaty

Library of Congress Catalogue Card No. 86-70789

ISBN 0-915361-58-2

Adama Books, 306 West 38th Street
New York, N.Y. 10018

Printed in Israel

contents:

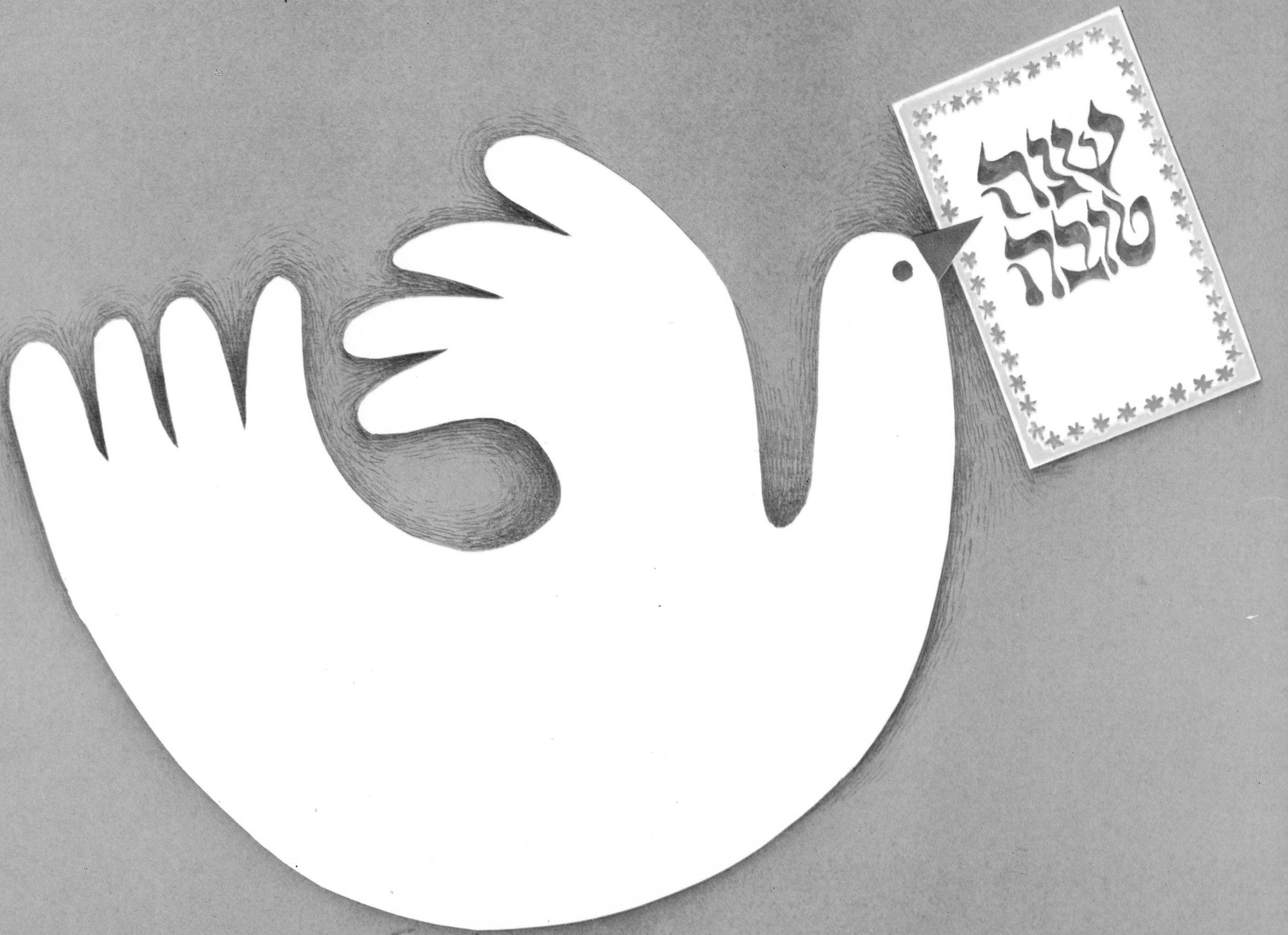
שנה
טובה

רֹאשׁ הַשָּׁנָה

For thirty days during the Hebrew month of Elul, Jews prepare themselves for the holidays to come. Each morning in their prayers they think about their behavior for the year just past. They think of any wrongs they may have done to their friends and relatives. They ask forgiveness from anyone they may have hurt, and just in case they may have hurt someone without realizing it, they ask everyone they know for forgiveness. They send cards with good wishes, saying, "May you be written down for a good year." Each morning during this special month, they hear the sound of the *shofar,* the ram's horn. It reminds them of the specialness of the time, and of the holy period that is about to arrive.

When Elul is over, the month of Tishri begins. The first ten days of Tishri are known as the High Holy Days. They are the most important days in the entire Jewish year. The first two days are Rosh Hashanah, the Jewish New Year. The last day is Yom Kippur, the Day of Atonement. The days between Rosh Hashanah and Yom Kippur are called the Days of Penitence.

Rosh Hashanah comes in the fall, usually in September or October. It starts a brand new calendar year for Jews. But Rosh Hashanah is not only the Jewish New Year; it is also what Jews call *Yom Hadin,* the Day of Judgment.

According to Jewish tradition, there is in heaven a symbolic book in which all of man's deeds are written. On one side are his good deeds and on the other, his bad. On Rosh Hashanah, Jews believe, God begins to study each and every man's behavior for the past year. Has he been a good person? Has he tried to be helpful? Has he hurt someone without knowing it? God studies all of man's actions. For the entire ten days of the High Holy Days, the heavenly book is kept open. As the sun goes down on Yom Kippur, God writes down, or inscribes what man's life will be like for the year to come.

Because man's fate is not sealed until the end of Yom Kippur, Jews spend the time from Rosh Hashanah onward trying to make themselves better people. They try to repent, which means they try to understand anything bad they may have done in their lives, and then try to change their ways.

They hope that by repenting, they will be written down for a better life. It is a very serious and very holy time.

Because Rosh Hashanah is such a holy time, Jews spend much of it in the synagogue praying. Many Jews wear simple white clothing to remind themselves of the holiness and purity of the time. The prayers, read from a special Rosh Hashanah prayer book, are old and beautiful and written like poems. Sometimes they are sung as songs. The same shofar which was sounded once each morning during the month of Elul is sounded more than 100 times during the two days of Rosh Hashanah. The long and short blasts are sharp and trill, and add to the very holy feeling of the period.

On Rosh Hashanah Jews read the portion of the Bible which tells of the sacrifice of Isaac. The story tells of how God commanded Abraham to take his son Isaac, his only son whom he loved very much, and to sacrifice him to God. Abraham had great faith in God, and prepared to follow His

command. He took the boy to a far off place, and built the altar as God had commanded. As he raised the knife, Abraham heard the voice of God tell him not to harm his son. He was to sacrifice an animal instead. As Abraham turned his head, he saw a ram caught by its horns among the thickets. This ram was to be Abraham's sacrifice to God. To this day, when Jews hear the shofar, which is the ram's horn, they remember Abraham's great faith in the ways of God.

There are many interesting customs for Rosh Hashanah. The special holiday bread called challah which is usually in the shape of a braid is for this holiday made round, like the snail's shell. This reminds people that the year goes around and around. It is also a custom to eat sweet things such as pieces of apple or challah dipped in honey. The honey is a symbol of a sweet year. It is also a custom to eat a new fruit of the season, and to say a prayer over it.

On the afternoon of the first day of Rosh Hashanah, Jews say special prayers called Tashlich near a running stream of water. When they have finished the prayers, they throw crumbs of bread into the water. They hope that like the crumbs, their evil ways will float away.

Apples dipped in *honey,* and *honey cake* are symbols of a sweet year.

New fruits of the season are blessed and eaten.

The shofar is made from the horn of a ram.

יוֹם כִּפּוּר

Day of Atonement • Yom Kippur

Yom Kippur comes exactly ten days after Rosh Hashanah. It is the holiest day of all the High Holy Days. On this day, Jews believe, God decides on the kind of life each man will have for the year to come.

On Rosh Hashanah, Jews believe, God opens a heavenly book. He looks at man's deeds for the year just past. For ten days, God studies man's deeds. On Yom Kippur, which is also known as the Day of Judgment, man's future is decided. The book is closed for another year.

Jews spend the ten days between Rosh Hashanah and Yom Kippur repenting for their sins. They try to understand their behavior, and anything wrong they may have done. They try to find ways to make themselves better people.

Yom Kippur is a fast day. On it, Jews eat no food and drink no water for twenty-five hours. They spend almost all their time in the synagogue. Fasting helps to keep their minds clear. They want to spend the entire time of Yom Kippur praying and repenting.

People come to the synagogue dressed in their best clothes. Some men wear a white robe, known as a kittel. The whiteness is a sign of purity. Many of the women wear white clothing, too.

During the Ten Days of Penitence between Rosh Hashanah and Yom Kippur, Jewish people ask for forgiveness from anyone they may have hurt. Jews believe they can only ask God's forgiveness after they have asked for man's. The Ten Days of Penitence give enemies a chance to become friends once again.

It is a Jewish custom, on the day before Yom Kippur, to take a chicken and swing it around the head three times while special prayers are said. The ceremony, known as *Kapparah,* is a very ancient ceremony. People long ago hoped that all their sins would be given over to the bird, and that any punishment they were to get would then also be given to the bird instead. Today, many people observe the ceremony of Kapparah with money instead of animals. After the ceremony the money is given to charity.

Yom Kippur begins, like all other Jewish holidays, in the evening.

It opens in the synagogue with the leader singing a prayer called *Kol Nidrei.* Jews read prayers from the Yom Kippur prayer book, and also begin to say prayers in their hearts and minds as well. They spend the entire time of the holiday thinking about their ways, thinking how they can become better people, praying that they will be forgiven for any wrongs they may have done. Many of the prayers are said out loud, with all the people in the synagogue joining in. The prayers ask God for forgiveness.

On the afternoon of Yom Kippur, the Bible story of the Prophet Jonah is read in the synagogue. The Prophet Jonah heard the voice of God. It told him to go to the wicked city of Nineveh. There, he was to tell the people to change their ways or they would be punished. Jonah refused. He ran from the voice of God. He ran to sea and was caught in a great storm. Jonah knew the storm came because God was angry with him. He told the sailors to throw him overboard, and the storm would end.

Jonah was thrown into the sea, and a great fish came and swallowed him. Jonah lived in the fish's belly where he prayed to God for forgiveness. After three days, the fish spit him out on the shores of Nineveh. Jonah did not want the people of Nineveh to be saved. Even so, he brought God's message to them. The people repented.

As Jonah sat in the hot sun, God made a tree grow. It protected Jonah from the sun. Jonah was pleased. Then a worm came and destroyed the tree. Jonah was very angry with God. "How can You have so little mercy on a tree," Jonah asked God. And God answered, "Shall I have mercy on a tree, and not on a whole nation of people?" The story of Jonah reminds Jews that God is eager for people to repent. If they repent, He will change His decree. He will write them down for a good year in the book of Life.

As the sun goes down on Yom Kippur, as the gates of heaven begin to close, Jews say the *Neilah* prayer, which is the holiest prayer of the Jews. And then, there is a long blast of the shofar. The holiday has come to an end. People go home to eat their first meal after the fast, and to prepare for the next holiday, Sukot, which comes in only four days.

15

סֻכּוֹת

Feast of Tabernacles • Sukot

For forty years after they escaped from slavery in Egypt, the Children of Israel wandered through the desert. They were waiting to receive the Ten Commandments from God and to be allowed to enter the Promised Land. Because they wandered from place to place, they did not bother to build permanent houses. Instead, during these forty years, the Children of Israel lived in temporary booths which they called *sukot*. These sukot could be easily built, and just as easily taken down.

When the Children of Israel entered the Promised Land, most of them became farmers. At the time of the harvest, they would go to the fields to cut their crops. Because the fields were far from their homes, and only donkeys and horses were used for transportation, the people would live in the fields for the entire period of the harvest. To protect themselves from the strong sun by day and from the cold and wind at night, the farmers built sukot.

The harvest was a time of celebration, a time to thank God for the goodness of the earth. When there was a Temple in Jerusalem, the people would bring the first fruits of their harvest to the priests in the Temple. They would bring it on foot, walking up to

Jerusalem. This was called a pilgrimage. It was one of the *Shalosh Regalim*. Today, although only very few Jews are farmers, Jews still celebrate the harvest each fall in a holiday called Sukot.

On Sukot, Jews do exactly what their ancestors did long ago. They leave the comfort of their homes, and for eight days they live in temporary booths that have no real roofs or doors. They eat, and sometimes even sleep in the sukot, remembering how their forefathers wandered through the desert, and how later on, in the Land of Israel, they harvested their crops and gave thanks to God.

The festival of Sukot comes exactly four days after Yom Kippur. It is a custom to begin building the sukah on the day following Yom Kippur. The sukah can be built anywhere — in back yards, on terraces, on roofs. The sukot are usually made from pieces of wood and cloth, and are decorated with pretty pictures and cut-outs, and hanging fruits which reminds us of

the harvest. The roofs of the sukot are usually of hay, or of branches of trees, so that at night, the stars shine through.

On Sukot, Jews make special prayers over the *lulav* and *etrog*. The lulav is a long palm branch around which have been wrapped branches of myrtle and willow. The etrog is a citron, which looks almost like a lemon. As the prayers are said, the lulav and etrog are waved in all directions.

The Wise Men of Israel say that the lulav represents the Jewish people. The palm tree, which has taste but no scent, is like the Jews who have learned all about Jewish law but do not do good deeds. The myrtle, which has smell but no taste, is like the Jews who do good deeds even though they do not know the law. The willow, which has no taste and no scent, is like the Jews who do not know the law and do not do good deeds. They are all bound together so that the good qualities of one will make up for the bad qualities of the other. The etrog

stands apart, because it has both taste and scent. It stands for those Jews who know the law and practice all the good deeds they can.

The sukah is a booth, usually covered with hay or branches of trees.

a   b

a) *The lulav* is a palm branch with twigs of myrtle and willow wrapped around it.
b) *The etrog* is a citron.

שִׂמְחַת תּוֹרָה

Festival of Rejoicing in the Law • Simchat Torah

The Torah scrolls, dressed in velvet and silver, are carried in circles around the synagogue.

Every week in synagogue, Jews read from their most special scroll. They read of the story of the creation of the world, of how the Jews were slaves to Pharaoh in Egypt, of how Moses received the Law from God on Mount Sinai, and how he then gave it to the Jewish people. And they also read the rules Moses gave them for living together in peace and kindness. On the holiday of Simchat Torah, the very last section of this special scroll is read.

This special scroll is called the Torah. Simchat Torah, which means rejoicing in the Law, is one of the gayest Jewish holidays, and is celebrated immediately after Sukot.

Torah scrolls in synagogues all over the world are dressed in velvet and silver and jewels for the holiday. After the final portion has been read, and special prayers have been said, people take the scrolls in their arms and dance in circles around the synagogue. The circles, called *Hakafot*, are very lively, and full of singing and merrymaking. Children with small Torah scrolls and flags, also join in.

Before the end of the holiday, the Torah scrolls are turned back to the beginning, all set to be read again. There really is no end to the Torah, Jews believe. Each time it is read, there is something new to be discovered.

Brightly-colored *flags* often with an apple and a lighted candle are carried by children on Simchat Torah.

חֲנֻכָּה

The Jews had been defeated by the Syrian king, Antiochus Epiphanes. He was a very cruel ruler. Although Antiochus was a Syrian, he followed the ways of the Greeks. He wanted the Jews to follow the ways of the Greeks, too. As much as they could, they refused to obey the king. The king was very angry.

On the twenty-fifth day of the Hebrew month of Kislev, the king ordered a new decree. He would force the Jews to obey his laws. From this time forward, he ordered, Jews were forbidden to read from their holy books. They were forbidden to pray to their God. They were forbidden to celebrate their holidays or the Sabbath. They were forbidden to observe any of the laws of their religion. Soldiers would make sure that the Jews observed these new laws. They would also set up pagan altars in the holiest Jewish place, the Temple. There the Jews would be made to sacrifice unclean animals to the Greek god Zeus. The Jews were horrified. But they were forced to obey the Syrians.

Syrian messengers went throughout the land telling the Jews of the king's decrees. When Mattathias, the priest of Modi'in, and his five sons, heard the bad news, they decided that something must be done. They could

26

not obey the king's orders. They ran to the hills, where they organized a small army. They were led by one of the brothers, Judah. They became known as the Maccabees. They fought for the freedom of their people.

For three years, Judah and the Maccabees fought against the Syrians. They fought on the mountains, and in the forests, and in the farmlands. After three years, on the twenty-fifth day of Kislev, the Maccabees were finally successful. They pushed the Syrian army out of their land. They were free people once again.

The Maccabees rushed for their holy Temple. They removed the pagan altar, and all the unclean animals. The *menorah,* the eight-branched candelabrum which was always to be burning in the Temple, was dark. They looked for the special, pure oil used to light it. It would take them eight days to make new oil. They searched and searched, but all they could find was one small cruse — enough oil to keep the menorah burning for one day.

The Maccabees lighted the menorah. They said special prayers of thanks to God. They thanked Him for bringing them to a time when they could be free men. And then, according to legend, a great miracle happened. The little cruse which had only enough oil to last for one day lasted for eight full days.

To remember the recapture of the Temple, and the miracle of the oil, Jews each year on the 25th of Kislev, which is in December, celebrate the holiday of Chanukah, which is also known as the Festival of Lights. Chanukah is celebrated for eight days, one for each day the oil burned.

A special menorah used for Chanukah can be found in many Jewish homes. This menorah, sometimes called a *chanukiyah,* is sometimes very old looking, and sometimes very modern. Sometimes it uses oil, and sometimes candles. Always, though, it has eight main branches, like the menorah lighted by the Maccabees in the Temple. For all of the eight days of Chanukah, the menorah is placed near a window so that all who pass can see its bright and beautiful glow.

On each night of Chanukah, the family gathers around the menorah. One light is lighted for each night — on the first night, one candle, on the second night two, and by the eighth night, eight lights are lighted. Special prayers are said over the lights, thanking God for the miracles He performed in the time of the Maccabees, and even now. Chanukah songs are sung by the entire family, telling of the great wonders that happened to the Maccabees long ago. One of the favorite songs is called *Maoz Tzur,* which means Rock of Ages. It sings praises to God, and also tells the story of the first Chanukah.

After the lighting of the lights, children usually play special gambling games, using a top called a dreidl or *sevivon.* On the sides of the dreidl are four Hebrew letters: Nun, Gimmel, Heh,

and Shin. These four letters stand for the words, *Nes Gadol Hayah Sham,* which means, A great miracle happened there. Each person playing the game starts off with a stash of raisins and almonds, and sometimes small money. Everyone places some of his stash in the center. Then each player in his turn starts to spin. If the dreidl falls on Gimmel, the player takes in the entire pot. If it is Heh, he takes half. If it is Nun, he takes nothing. And if it is Shin, he must put something extra into the pot.

While the children are playing dreidl, there are usually wonderful smells wafting through the house. Chanukah is a time for latkes, special potato pancakes, which are also called *levivot.* Many people also eat jelly-filled doughnuts called *savganiot.*

Chanukah is also a time for giving presents. Some parents give their children one or two presents for the holiday, and some give a different present for each of the eight nights of the holiday.

The Festival of Lights has a very special meaning in Israel. There, every year at the start of Chanukah, a torch is lighted in Modi'in, the home of the Maccabees, and is carried by runners all the way to the home of the president, many miles away. The torch reminds the Israelis of the lights of freedom, in days past and even today.

The menorah is the symbol of the miracle of Chanukah. *The cruse* found in the Temple contained oil for only one day. It lasted for eight.

Sevivon or dreidl is a special chanukah top sometimes played for money and sometimes for *nuts.*

Latkes are potato pancakes eaten on Chanukah.
Savganiot are jelly doughnuts eaten on Chanukah.

Feast of Lots • Purim

There is one day in the year when Jewish children can be seen walking around in costumes of kings and queens and villains, wearing masks and twirling noisemakers and carrying baskets of fruits and cakes. This day usually comes some time in March, on the fourteenth day of the Hebrew month of Adar. It is known as Purim and it is one of the merriest days in the Jewish year.

The story of Purim is written in the Bible. It is called *Megillat Esther,* the Scroll of Esther. Long ago, the story says, in the ancient kingdom of Persia, in the capital city of Shushan, there lived a king by the name of Ahasuerus. King Ahasuerus was very rich and his kingdom spread over 127 countries. He was a happy king, and he liked to give great parties.

Once Ahasuerus made a feast that lasted for days and days. All the great people in the kingdom were invited. When the feast was almost over, the king asked that Queen Vashti be brought to him. When Vashti refused, the king ordered her sent away from the kingdom. After the feasting was over, the king became very lonely. A king must have a queen, he said to himself. I will find another, more beautiful woman than Vashti and make her my queen. The king ordered his servants to issue a proclamation. There was to be a great beauty pageant. The most beautiful girl in the pageant he would take for his new queen.

All the girls in the kingdom wanted to become queen — all except one by the name of Esther. Even so, she was the most beautiful of all the girls, and Ahasuerus chose her to be his new queen. The king did not know that Esther was Jewish, and Esther did not tell him.

Because Ahasuerus was always busy giving parties, he had very little time to rule his kingdom. This he left to his chief advisor, a man by the man of Haman. Because Haman was wicked, the people obeyed his orders. Only one man, Mordecai the Jew, refused to obey Haman. Mordecai was also Queen Esther's cousin.

Haman became very angry with Mordecai, and with all the Jews. He decided to have them killed. Haman cast lots, or *purim,* to choose a date for the killing. The lots fell on the thirteenth day of the month of Adar. Haman asked for the king's seal on the decree, and the king agreed. Haman's plan was all set.

When word of the decree reached Mordecai, he rushed to the palace to see his cousin the queen. It was time, Mordecai said, for Esther to tell the king she was Jewish, and to beg him to save her people. Esther was afraid the king would have her killed. She could see the king only if he called her. Finally, Esther agreed to speak to the king.

For three days the Jews of the kingdom prayed for Esther's success. Then Esther went to the king. The king was pleased and held out his scepter to her; she would not be killed. The king offered Esther anything she wanted, even half of his kingdom. All she wanted, she said, was that the king and Haman join her for dinner the following evening. It was agreed.

At the same time, Mordecai saved the king's life. While sitting at the palace gates, he overheard some servants planning to murder the king. Mordecai informed the king, and was written down in the book of good deeds. One night, when the king could not sleep, he read his book and remembered he had done nothing to thank Mordecai. He ordered Haman sent in.

The king told Haman he should like to give special honor to one of his subjects. Haman decided the king was speaking of him. So he suggested that this man be dressed in the king's very own robes and crown, and that he be seated on the king's very own royal steed. He should then be led through the streets of Shushan by the king's own guard. The king's face lit up. A splendid idea.

When the king told Haman it was Mordecai

the Jew who was to be honored, Haman flew into a rage. He had special gallows built for Mordecai wich were to be used on the thirteenth day of the month of Adar. Even so, Haman had to lead Mordecai through the streets of Shushan calling, ''Thus shall be done to the man the king delights to honor.''

Esther made ready for her banquet. And when the king and Haman arrived, Ahasuerus once again offered Esther anything she wanted, even half of his kingdom. All she wanted, Esther said, was that the king and Haman join her again for another banquet the next evening. It was agreed.

The next evening, the king again offered Esther anything she wanted. And this time Esther said that she wanted her life spared and the lives of her people. She told Ahasuerus she was Jewish and that the wicked Haman was about to have all the Jews killed. Ahasuerus became very angry. He ordered Haman hanged on the very gallows he had prepared for Mordecai. The Jews were saved, and they held a great feast to celebrate.

Jews today celebrate Purim by reading the *Megillah* or Scroll of Esther. Every time the name Haman is mentioned, people stamp their feet and twirl noisemakers to drown out the sound of the name Children dress up in costumes and put on plays that retell the story of the holiday. People send gifts called *mishloach manot* and eat special three-cornered cakes called hamantaschen. These cakes are the shape of Haman's three-cornered hat and are usually filled with prunes or poppyseeds.

Megillah, scroll, or rolled up paper, sometimes made of parchment. Long ago scrolls were used for writing books and for sending out proclamations.

Hamantaschen, three-cornered cakes in the shape of Haman's hat, usually filled with prunes or poppyseeds.

Masks and costumes help to retell the Purim story.

Passover • Pesach

For many years, the Children of Israel had been slaves to Pharaoh in Egypt. The taskmasters were cruel and forced them to work harder and harder. They were building the great pyramid storehouses of Pithom and Ramses. As they worked in the hot sun, they remembered a better time, before they had become slaves.

The Children of Israel had come to live in Egypt when Joseph, their brother, was prime minister. They had come, seventy people in all, and settled in the city of Goshen. There they lived and worked as free people. They had many children and became a large nation. They were happy in Egypt.

A new Pharaoh come to rule over Egypt. He was frightened of the Children of Israel. He thought that perhaps they would go to war against Egypt. He issued a cruel decree. All their newborn sons would be killed. All the Hebrews were to become slaves.

At this time, a son was born to a Hebrew by the name of Yocheved. She did not kill her son. Her daughter Miriam was to set the child afloat in a basket on the River Nile. She was to watch over it and make sure it was safe. The basket was found by Pharaoh's daughter who took the child home and adopted him as her own son. She called the child Moses.

As Moses grew up, he saw the suffering of the Hebrews. It made him angry. Once, Moses saw an Egyptian beating a Hebrew slave. He killed the Egyptian and ran away.

Moses became a shepherd in the land of Midian. There, while tending his sheep, he came across a bush. It was burning, but it did not turn to ash. From the bush Moses heard the voice of God. It told him to go to Pharaoh and tell him that the God of the Hebrews said to free His people from slavery.

Many times, Moses went to Pharaoh. Always, Pharaoh agreed to let the Children of Israel leave. Always he went back on his word. Many plagues were brought upon the Egyptians — blood, wild animals, hailstones. With each plague, Pharaoh said the Hebrews could leave. When the plague was gone, he changed his mind again.

Finally, Moses told Pharaoh that if he did not let the Hebrews go, a tenth plague would be brought on the

Egyptians. All the firstborn sons would be killed. Pharaoh was frightened. He was the eldest in his family. He told Moses to take his people and leave the land of Egypt.

Moses told the Children of Israel to prepare themselves. They were to sacrifice a lamb, and paint some of its blood on the doorposts of their homes. The Angel of Death was to come and kill all firstborn Egyptians. He would pass over the homes whose doorposts were painted with blood. They did as Moses said. Quickly they prepared bread for the journey. But before the bread had time to rise, they were already on their way. When he saw them leaving, Pharaoh once again changed his mind.

The large nation of slaves followed Moses. They walked until they reached the Red Sea. There, Moses took his rod and touched it to the water. A great miracle happened. The water spread apart so that the Children of Israel could pass on dry land. As the Egyptians came up behind, Moses once again touched the water with his rod. The waters returned, and the Egyptians and their chariots were drowned in the sea. The Children of Israel sang songs of joy. They were free men once again.

To celebrate this freedom, each year Jews observe the holiday of Pesach, which is called Passover in English. The holiday of Pesach begins on the fourteenth day of the Hebrew month of Nisan, which is sometime in April or May. Some people celebrate the holiday for seven days, and some for eight.

On Pesach Jews eat no bread. Many clean out their entire homes so that no trace of bread is left. By the first night of Pesach, the house is usually spotlessly clean. The table is set in preparation for the *seder,* the retelling of the story of Pesach.

The family gathers around the table. The seder is about to begin. Each place is set with a special booklet called a *hagadah,* and with a wine goblet.

The youngest child opens the seder with four questions. "Why", he begins, "is this night different from all other nights? Why on all other nights do we eat all kinds of bread, and on this night we eat only matzah?" When he has completed his questions, the head of the house reads the answers from the hagadah. "Because we were slaves in Egypt" he begins. "And now we are free men." The retelling of the story begins.

During the seder, each person drinks four cups of wine. He eats bitter herbs called *maror,* to remind him of the bitterness of slavery. He eats a special apple and nut paste called *charoset,* to remind him of the bricks used in building the pyramids. He dips vegetables in salt water to remind him of the tears shed by the Hebrew slaves. Many of these foods are placed together on one plate, along with a roasted bone, which reminds people of the lamb sacrificed in Egypt. On the table, too, are three *matzot* — the flat bread quickly baked by the Children of Israel as they rushed from Egypt.

During the reading of the hagadah, many songs are sung and interesting stories told. A special cup of wine is poured for the Prophet Elijah, who, it is thought, comes to visit each Jewish home on this night.

As the seder comes to an end, people eat a last piece of matzah known as the *afikomen* and thank God for His very special gift of freedom.

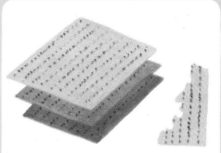

Matzah is unleavened bread.

The seder plate has a roasted bone, bitter herbs, charoset, parsley, and a roasted egg.

The Hagadah tells the story of Pesach.

At the seder each person drinks *four cups* of wine.

The cup of Elijah is set on the table.

A pitcher and *basin* are used to wash hands twice during the seder.

יוֹם הָעַצְמָאוּת

When the Romans conquered the Land of Israel, many Jews were taken away as slaves. They were scattered all over the world — in Europe, in Africa, in Asia, and later in the Americas, too. The Jews were in exile in strange lands. Sometimes, they were well accepted in the countries in which they lived. Most of the time, though, they had to pay high taxes, and wear special clothes, and live in separate sections of towns. They were beaten, and robbed, and even killed. Wherever they lived, always in their hopes and their dreams, they remembered their land. Always, they spoke of returning to it. Next year in Jerusalem was forever on their lips.

At the very beginning of the twentieth century, at a time when the Jews of Europe were having a very difficult time, a new movement called Zionism was born. The head of the movement, Theodor Herzl, believed that the Jewish people should live in a land of its own. He called meetings of great Jewish leaders from all over the world. He told them, ''Perhaps not in five years, but in fifty, there will be a Jewish state. If you will it — it is no dream.''

The fifty years that followed this first Zionist meeting were probably the worst in all of Jewish history. Many millions of Jews were killed by the

Nazis during the Second World War. The British were in control of the Land of Israel, which was then called Palestine. Jews who escaped from the Nazis and came to Palestine were sent away. Many people tried to sneak into the country in the middle of the night. Sometimes, the British sunk the ships and many people drowned. Even so, the population of Palestine grew and grew.

In 1947, the United Nations voted to establish a national homeland for Jews. On May 14, 1948, David Ben Gurion, the first Prime Minister of Israel, read the Declaration of Independence of the New State. The Hebrew date was the fifth of Iyar. The Jewish people in the country went wild with joy. They danced and sang and cried. Jews all over the world shared their joy. It was the first Yom Ha-Atzmaut, the first Israel Independence Day. After 2,000 years, the Jews had come home.

Each year on Yom Ha-Atzmaut, Israelis gather together around bonfires to sing and dance and watch fireworks. They tell stories of the founding of the country and of the pioneers who helped to build it. And they remember all those who died fighting for independence in Israel's four wars with its Arab neighbors.

The flag of Israel is blue stripes on white, with a star of David in the center.

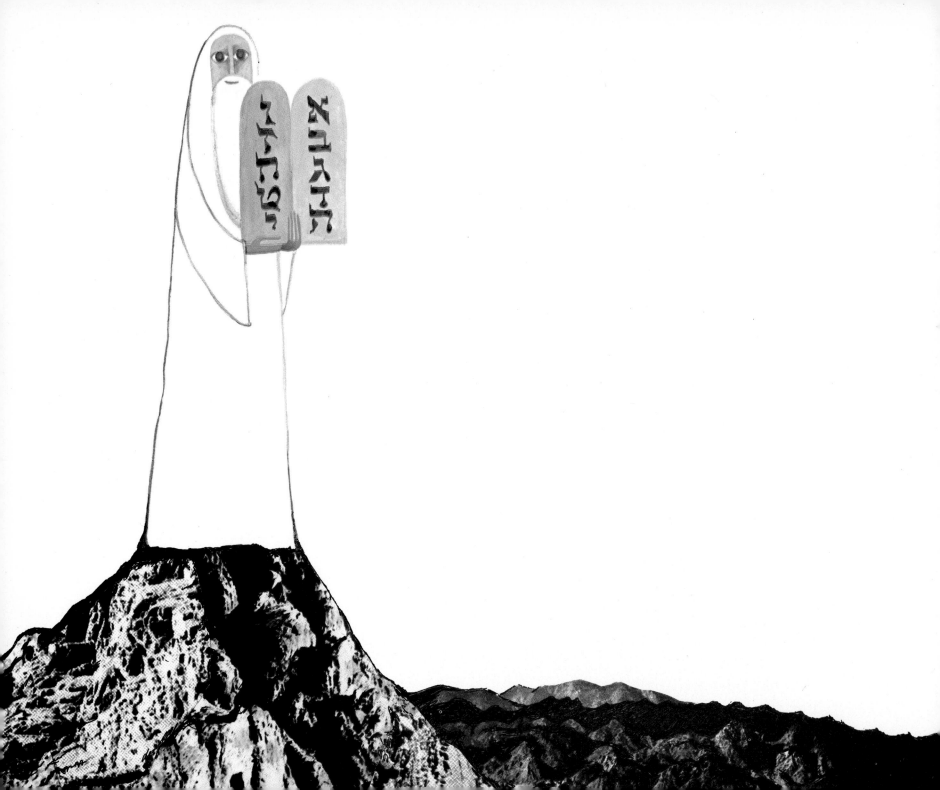

שָׁבוּעוֹת

Many years ago, a legend says,
God decided to give His Law to man.
God went to the people of Ammon.
"Do you want My Law," God asked.
And the people of Amon said, "First
tell us what is written in it." When
God told them His Law said, "You must
not kill," the people of Ammon said,
"No, that is not the kind of Law for us."

Next God went to the people of Moab.
"Do you want My Law," God asked.
And the people of Moab said,
"First tell us what is written in it."
When God told them His Law said,
"You must not steal," the people of
Moab said, "No, that is not the kind
of Law for us."

God went from nation to nation, from
people to people. Each one God asked,
"Do you want My Law?" And each
one said, "First tell us what is written
in it." When God had told them His
Laws for living together in peace,
they all said, "No, that is not the kind
of Law for us." Finally, the legend
says, God came to a very small nation
who had just escaped from slavery in
Egypt. They were known as the
Children of Israel. "Do you want My
Law," God asked. And the Children
of Israel answered, "Yes, we do. Now
tell us what is written in Your Law."

And so God gathered the Children of
Israel at Mount Sinai. He called Moses,

their leader, to the top of the mountain. There He taught Moses the Ten Commandments for living together in peace. These Laws were written on two tablets of stone called *luchot*. When Moses came down the mountain, he taught the Children of Israel all the Laws in God's commandments. These Laws were the Torah. They said,

- **There is only one God**
- **Do not bow down to idols**
- **Do not swear falsely by the name of God**
- **Keep the Sabbath holy**
- **Honor your father and mother**
- **Do not murder**
- **Do not take another man's wife, or another woman's husband**
- **Do not steal**
- **Do not lie**
- **Do not want what does not belong to you.**

The Children of Israel learned God's Laws. And they obeyed them. And to remember this most important happening in their history, Jews forever after have celebrated the festival of Shavuot.

But the giving of the Torah at Mount Sinai is only part of the reason for Shavuot. After the Children of Israel left Sinai, they entered the Promised Land, the Land of Israel. There they settled down and most people became farmers. In order to thank God for giving them good harvests, the people would go by foot, three times a year, up to the holy city of Jerusalem, to the Temple, to bring God's priests, the *Kohanim*, a part of their harvests. These three times were called the *Shalosh Regalim*, or pilgrimages. Shavuot, which comes at the time of the spring harvest, is one of the Shalosh Regalim.

Shavuot comes exactly seven weeks after the holiday of Pesach, on the sixth day of the Hebrew month of Sivan. Many Jews in Israel and Jews all over the world celebrate the holiday by decorating their homes with beautiful flowers and leaves which remind them of the spring harvest. It is also a custom to eat meals of dairy products such as cheese and eggs. Many people eat special

pancakes filled with cheese, called blintzes.

On Shavuot, Jews go to synagogue and thank God for giving them the Torah. They also read a book from the Bible called the Book of Ruth. This book tells the story of a young Moabite woman who left her land and her people to go with her Jewish mother-in-law to the Land of Israel.
The story takes place at the time of the spring harvest, and tells of Ruth's strong love and faith.

Shavuot is also a time when some Jews begin to give their children a Jewish education. By beginning to teach their children the Torah, they feel they too are standing at the foot of Mount Sinai, helping their children to receive God's Law.

Firstborn animals were brought to God's priests in the Temple.

The Torah tells God's Laws, and also the early history of the Children of Israel. It is written on a scroll and has five parts.

Bikurim, the first fruits of the harvest, were brought to God's priests in the Temple.

Flowers decorate Jewish homes to remind people of the harvest.

The Luchot, the Ten Commandments, were written on two stone tablets. The commandments are written in the Torah.

The Harvest was a time when Jews thanked God for the food of the Earth.

תִּשְׁעָה בְּאָב

Ninth of Av • Tisha B'Av

The Romans were at the gates of Jerusalem. Their catapults sent large round stones crashing into homes and shops. There was no food and no water. It had been a long battle, and the Jews were weak from hunger and thirst. When they saw their Holy Temple go up in flames, they knew the end had come. Their city would be completely destroyed, and they would be taken as slaves to Rome. The day was Tisha B'Av, the ninth day of the Hebrew month of Av. It was the saddest day in all of Jewish history. The Jews were sent from the land. They were in exile.

Wherever they were whether in Europe, or Africa, or later, in the New World, Jews put aside the ninth day of Av as a day of mourning. Tisha B'Av is a fast day. From sundown to sundown, Jews eat no food and drink no water. When they enter the synagogue, they remove their shoes and sit on low stools, or on overturned benches, or even on the floor. Just as when they are in mourning for the death of a relative, they do not say hello or goodbye. The Ark of Law is usually draped with black cloth, and the only light comes from the *ner tamid,* the eternal light that always burns in the synagogue.

On Tisha B'Av, Jews read from the Book of Lamentations. This book tells about the destruction of the First Temple. It is a long, sad poem — the kind of poem people read when someone has died. Other poems, called *Kinnot,* are also read. The Kinnot tell of other sad events in Jewish history.

שַׁבָּת

Sabbath • Shabbat

In six days, the Bible says, God created the sun and the moon and the stars, and the fish that swim in the seas, and the plants and flowers that grow on dry land, and the birds that fly, and all the wild and gentle animals that live on earth. When He had finished all His other creations, God created man and woman, and He called them Adam and Eve. As the sun set on the sixth day after He had begun to create, God rested from all His work. All that He had created rested, too. It was the first Shabbat, the first Sabbath. It was a very peaceful, very holy time.

Jews celebrate Shabbat each week on Friday night and all day Saturday.

They remember the first Sabbath, and are obeying the fourth of the Ten Commandments which says, "Six days shall you labor and do all your work. But the seventh day is a sabbath to the Lord your God. You shall not do any manner of work for the Lord blessed the sabbath day and hallowed it."

שַׁבָּת שָׁלוֹם

A good Sabbath.

Not all Jews understand this commandment in the same way, and

not all Jews celebrate the Sabbath exactly alike. Some people understand the law very strictly. They do not work, or cook, or drive in cars, or put on lights. Other people understand the law to mean that Shabbat is a day for rest and relaxation. But however they interpret the commandment, there are many, many customs shared by all.

By late Friday afternoon, the Sabbath table is set with a snowy white cloth and the best dishes, with wine and a wine goblet, two loaves of sweet, braided Sabbath bread called *challot,* and with candlesticks. As the sun begins to set, the woman of the house welcomes the Sabbath with the blessing of the candles. The house is all aglow as the family leaves for services in the synagogue.

When the family returns from synagogue, the Sabbath meal begins. Before eating dinner, the wine goblet is filled to brimming. The man of the house raises the cup and recites the special blessing over the wine called *Kiddush.* Kiddush means "to make

holy." By reciting this blessing, Jews remember that the Sabbath is a holy time. Everyone tastes the wine, and by doing this becomes holy, too. A blessing is made over the challot and the meal begins. Fish, soup, chicken, and puddings made from noodles and potatoes are Shabbat favorites. During the meal, the family sings Sabbath songs called *zemirot.* The verses of these songs are hundreds of years old but the tunes are usually modern.

On Shabbat morning, the family attends services in the synagogue once again. During this service, the Torah scroll is removed from the ark and is read. After services, the kiddush is recited once again.

On Saturday evening, when three stars can be seen in the sky, a special ceremony known as *Havdalah* helps to separate the Sabbath from the rest of the week. A wine goblet is filled and raised, a braided candle with many wicks is lighted, a sweet-smelling box of spices is passed from person to

Candles are lighted to welcome the Sabbath.

A special blessing called *kiddush* is said over the wine.

Challot are special Sabbath loaves.

A twisted candle and *spices* from a spice box are used to make the Havdalah.

person, and a special blessing is said thanking God for the Sabbath and for separating the holy from the ordinary. A new week has started.

שָׁבוּעַ טוֹב

A happy week.

Now you will discover how clever you are!
You will find symbols and utensils on the following two pages are used throughout the Jewish year.

Look for the symbols belonging to a holiday. Next to the symbol you will find a printed number. In the space provided on the next page, write down the number and next to it the name and/or the action of each symbol or utensil.

For example, for Shabbat you have to do the following:

1 **(21)** Candles
2 **(28)** Kiddush
3 **(10)** Challot
4 **(15)** Havdalah candle
5 **(18)** Spice box

You must write with a pencil so that you can erase and use the space again. Isn't this a nice game to play with your friends?

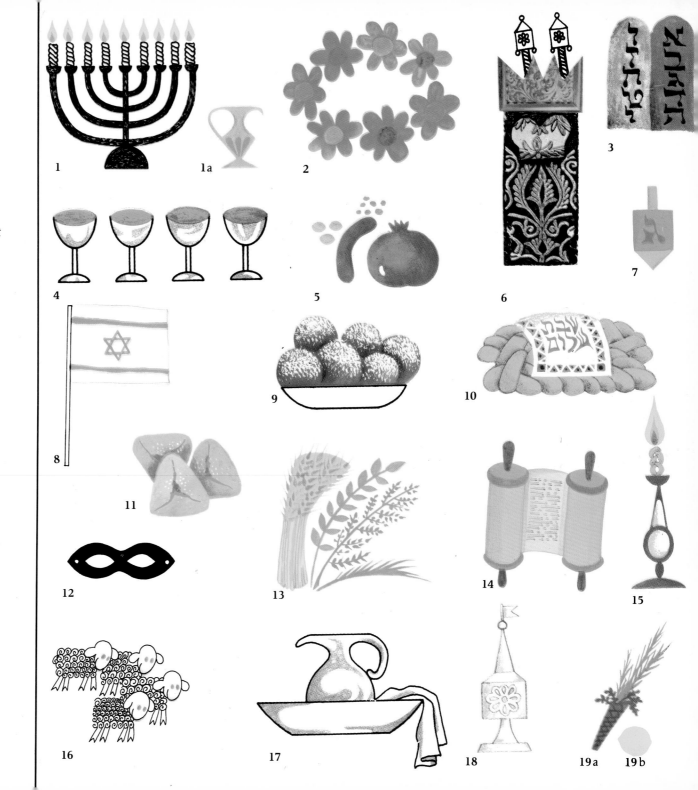

Rosh Hashanah

1 _____
2 _____
3 _____

Sukot

1 _____
2 _____

Simchat Torah

1 _____
2 _____

Chanukah

1 _____
2 _____
3 _____
4 _____

Purim

1 _____
2 _____
3 _____

Pesach

1 _____
2 _____
3 _____
4 _____
5 _____
6 _____

Yom Ha-Atzmaut

1 _____

Shavuot

1 _____
2 _____
3 _____
4 _____
5 _____
6 _____

Shabbat

1 _____
2 _____
3 _____
4 _____
5 _____

20

21

22

23

24

25

26

27

28

28

29

30

31

31

31

32